anythink

D0618361

Sea Stars

BY KARA L. LAUGHLIN

The Child's World®
childsworld.com

Published by The Child's World®
1980 Lookout Drive • Mankato, MN 56003-1705
800-599-READ • www.childsworld.com

DESIGN ELEMENTS
© creatOR76/Shutterstock.com: porthole
© keren-seg/Shutterstock.com: water

PHOTO CREDITS
© D.P. Wilson/FLPA/Minden Pictures: 18-19; Ethan Daniels/
Shutterstock.com: 11; Georgia Walters/Shutterstock.com:
14; Jason Mintzer/Shutterstock.com: 6-7; Kondratuk Aleksei/
Shutterstock.com: 8-9; Paul Atkinson/Shutterstock.com: 5;
Seaphotoart/Shutterstock.com: cover, 1, 20-21; Tiago Sa Brito/
Shutterstock.com: 12-13; Wim van Egmond: 17

ISBN: 9781503816930
LCCN: 2016945659

Printed in the United States of America
PA02326

NOTE FOR PARENTS AND TEACHERS

The Child's World® helps early readers develop their
informational-reading skills by providing easy-to-read books
that fascinate them and hold their interest. Encourage new
readers by following these simple ideas:

BEFORE READING

• Page briefly through the book. Discuss the photos. What
  does the reader think he or she will learn in this book? Let
  the child ask questions.
• Look at the glossary together. Discuss the words.

READ THE BOOK

• Now read the book together, or let the child read the book
  independently.

AFTER READING

• Urge the child to think more. Ask questions such as, "What
  things are different among the animals shown in this book?"

Contents

Stars of All Colors

What is that animal on that rock? It is a sea star. Sea stars are also called starfish. They come in lots of colors. Some are dull. Others are bright.

Did you know?

Sea stars live only in salty water.

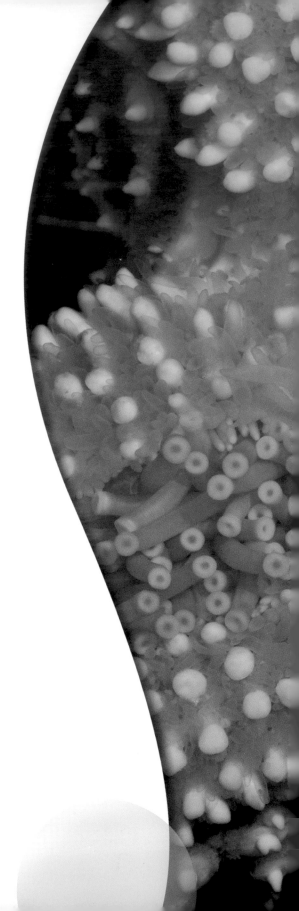

Tubes for Feet

Many sea stars
have five legs.
Some have many
more. Under each
leg are **tube feet**.

Did you know?

Sea stars do not have a brain.

On top, sea stars have bumpy skin. They also have a dot called a **sieve plate**. It pulls water into the sea star.

sieve plate

Sea stars need water like other animals need blood.

Did you know?

Some sea stars grow larger than a manhole cover.

Eyes on Their Legs

Sea stars have an eye at the end of each leg. These eyes sense light. Sea stars cannot see shapes or colors.

Did you know?

Sea stars live in every ocean in the world.

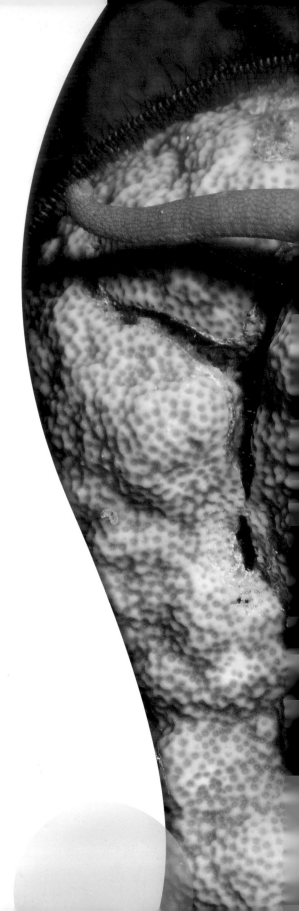

Growing New Legs

If a sea star loses a leg, it can grow a new one. This is called **regeneration**.

Did you know?

Not many animals eat sea stars.

Inside-Out Eating

A sea star uses an odd trick when it eats. It pushes its stomach out of its body. This helps sea stars eat things that are big or hard to reach.

Did you know?

Sea stars eat things such as clams, mussels, and snails.

A Sea Star is Born

Sea stars **spawn**. They release eggs or sperm into the sea. When an egg and a sperm meet, they grow into a **larva**. The larva does not look like a sea star.

Did you know?

Sea stars do not have blood.

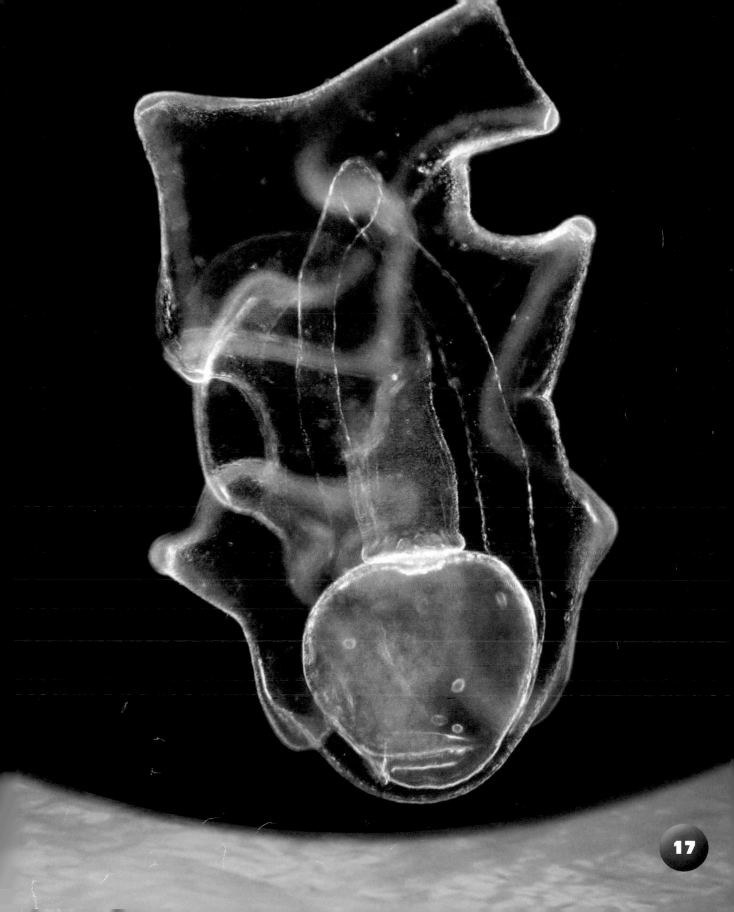

Did you know?

Sea stars do not have bones.

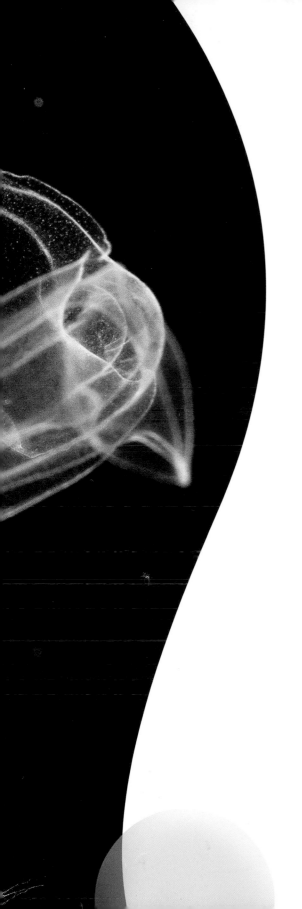

Sea stars undergo **metamorphosis**. Their bodies change from being like bugs to being like sea stars.

Sea stars are strange and beautiful creatures in the sea!

Did you know?

Sea stars live for about 35 years.

21

GLOSSARY

larva (LAR-vuh): A baby sea star is called a larva. It looks more like a bug than a sea star.

metamorphosis (met-uh-MOR-fuh-sis): When an animal's body changes from one shape to a different shape as it becomes an adult. (Caterpillars go through metamorphosis to become butterflies.)

regeneration (ree-jen-ur-AY-shun): Regeneration is growing back a body part.

sieve plate (SIV PLAYT): The bump on top of a sea star that lets water into its body is a sieve plate.

spawn (SPAWN): When animals spawn, they let lots of eggs or sperm out of their bodies at once so that lots of baby animals can grow.

tube feet (TOOB FEET): Tube feet are the tiny, bendy tubes on the underside of a sea star. Tube feet help with eating, moving, and breathing.

TO LEARN MORE

on the Web

Visit our Web page for
lots of links about sea stars:
www.childsworld.com/links

Note to parents, teachers, and librarians:
We routinely verify our Web links to make
sure they are safe, active sites—
so encourage your readers
to check them out!

In the Library

Barroux. *Starfish, Where Are You?* New York, NY:
Little Bee Books, 2016.

Halfmann, Janet. *Star of the Sea: A Day in the Life of a Starfish.*
New York, NY: Henry Holt, 2011.

Kenan, Tessa. *Look, A Starfish!* Minneapolis, MN:
Lerner Publications, 2017.

INDEX

About the Author

Kara L. Laughlin is an artist and writer who lives in Virginia with her husband, three kids, two guinea pigs, and a dog. She is the author of two dozen nonfiction books for kids.